Renascence & Other Poems by Edna St Vincent Millay

Edna St. Vincent Millay was born on 22nd February 1892 in Rockland, Maine, the eldest of three daughters.

Her early years were tinted with much difficulty; divorced parents, poverty and a constant change of location.

Despite this once settled in Camden, Maine Edna developed her literary talents at a furious rate. By 15, she had published her poetry in the popular children's magazine St. Nicholas, the Camden Herald, and the high-profile anthology Current Literature.

In 1912, at 20, she entered her poem 'Renascence' in The Lyric Year poetry contest. Despite being considered the best poem it was only given fourth place. The ensuing uproar brought publicity and the offer of funding for her education at Vassar College. Here she wrote, both verse and plays as well as embarking on a series of affairs with women as she explored the wider world and all it offered.

Edna achieved significant fame when she won the Pulitzer Prize for Poetry in 1923 for 'The Ballad of the Harp-Weaver'. It was a magnificent triumph.

She married Eugen Jan Boissevain but on her wedding day she fell ill and he drove her to Manhattan for emergency surgery. He nursed her back to health with remarkable devotion. They were together, in an open marriage, until his death in 1949.

In the summer of 1936, Edna was riding in a station wagon when the door swung open and she was hurled into the pitch-darkness and rolled into a rocky gully. She survived but with severely damaged nerves in her spine and was to live the rest of her life in pain.

In 1942 in an article for The New York Times Magazine, Edna mourned the callous destruction of the Czechoslovak town of Lidice by Nazi forces in retaliation for the assassination of Reinhard Heydrich. The article would serve as the basis of her 32-page poem, 'Murder of Lidice' in 1942.

Edna St. Vincent Millay, after suffering a heart attack, fell down the stairs and died at her home on 19th October 1950. She was 58 years old.

Index of Poems

I0163460

Renascence

All I could see from where I stood
Was three long mountains and a wood;
I turned and looked another way,
And saw three islands in a bay.
So with my eyes I traced the line
Of the horizon, thin and fine,
Straight around till I was come
Back to where I'd started from;
And all I saw from where I stood
Was three long mountains and a wood.
Over these things I could not see;
These were the things that bounded me;
And I could touch them with my hand,
Almost, I thought, from where I stand.
And all at once things seemed so small
My breath came short, and scarce at all.
But, sure, the sky is big, I said;
Miles and miles above my head;
So here upon my back I'll lie
And look my fill into the sky.
And so I looked, and, after all,
The sky was not so very tall.
The sky, I said, must somewhere stop,
And—sure enough!—I see the top!
The sky, I thought, is not so grand;
I 'most could touch it with my hand!
And reaching up my hand to try,
I screamed to feel it touch the sky.
I screamed, and—lo!—Infinity
Came down and settled over me;
Forced back my scream into my chest,
Bent back my arm upon my breast,
And, pressing of the Undefined
The definition on my mind,
Held up before my eyes a glass
Through which my shrinking sight did pass

Until it seemed I must behold
Immensity made manifold;
Whispered to me a word whose sound
Deafened the air for worlds around,
And brought unmuffled to my ears
The gossiping of friendly spheres,
The creaking of the tented sky,
The ticking of Eternity.
I saw and heard, and knew at last
The How and Why of all things, past,
And present, and forevermore.
The Universe, cleft to the core,
Lay open to my probing sense
That, sick'ning, I would fain pluck thence
But could not,—nay! But needs must suck
At the great wound, and could not pluck
My lips away till I had drawn
All venom out.—Ah, fearful pawn!
For my omniscience paid I toll
In infinite remorse of soul.
All sin was of my sinning, all
Atoning mine, and mine the gall
Of all regret. Mine was the weight
Of every brooded wrong, the hate
That stood behind each envious thrust,
Mine every greed, mine every lust.
And all the while for every grief,
Each suffering, I craved relief
With individual desire,—
Craved all in vain! And felt fierce fire
About a thousand people crawl;
Perished with each,—then mourned for all!
A man was starving in Capri;
He moved his eyes and looked at me;
I felt his gaze, I heard his moan,
And knew his hunger as my own.
I saw at sea a great fog bank
Between two ships that struck and sank;
A thousand screams the heavens smote;
And every scream tore through my throat.
No hurt I did not feel, no death
That was not mine; mine each last breath
That, crying, met an answering cry
From the compassion that was I.
All suffering mine, and mine its rod;
Mine, pity like the pity of God.
Ah, awful weight! Infinity
Pressed down upon the finite Me!

My anguished spirit, like a bird,
Beating against my lips I heard;
Yet lay the weight so close about
There was no room for it without.
And so beneath the weight lay I
And suffered death, but could not die.

Long had I lain thus, craving death,
When quietly the earth beneath
Gave way, and inch by inch, so great
At last had grown the crushing weight,
Into the earth I sank till I
Full six feet under ground did lie,
And sank no more,—there is no weight
Can follow here, however great.
From off my breast I felt it roll,
And as it went my tortured soul
Burst forth and fled in such a gust
That all about me swirled the dust.

Deep in the earth I rested now;
Cool is its hand upon the brow
And soft its breast beneath the head
Of one who is so gladly dead.
And all at once, and over all
The pitying rain began to fall;
I lay and heard each pattering hoof
Upon my lowly, thatched roof,
And seemed to love the sound far more
Than ever I had done before.
For rain it hath a friendly sound
To one who's six feet underground;
And scarce the friendly voice or face:
A grave is such a quiet place.

The rain, I said, is kind to come
And speak to me in my new home.
I would I were alive again
To kiss the fingers of the rain,
To drink into my eyes the shine
Of every slanting silver line,
To catch the freshened, fragrant breeze
From drenched and dripping apple-trees.
For soon the shower will be done,
And then the broad face of the sun
Will laugh above the rain-soaked earth
Until the world with answering mirth
Shakes joyously, and each round drop

Rolls, twinkling, from its grass-blade top.
How can I bear it; buried here,
While overhead the sky grows clear
And blue again after the storm?
O, multi-colored, multiform,
Beloved beauty over me,
That I shall never, never see
Again! Spring-silver, autumn-gold,
That I shall never more behold!
Sleeping your myriad magics through,
Close-sepulchred away from you!
O God, I cried, give me new birth,
And put me back upon the earth!
Upset each cloud's gigantic gourd
And let the heavy rain, down-poured
In one big torrent, set me free,
Washing my grave away from me!

I ceased; and through the breathless hush
That answered me, the far-off rush
Of herald wings came whispering
Like music down the vibrant string
Of my ascending prayer, and—crash!
Before the wild wind's whistling lash
The startled storm-clouds reared on high
And plunged in terror down the sky,
And the big rain in one black wave
Fell from the sky and struck my grave.
I know not how such things can be;
I only know there came to me
A fragrance such as never clings
To aught save happy living things;
A sound as of some joyous elf
Singing sweet songs to please himself,
And, through and over everything,
A sense of glad awakening.
The grass, a-tiptoe at my ear,
Whispering to me I could hear;
I felt the rain's cool finger-tips
Brushed tenderly across my lips,
Laid gently on my sealed sight,
And all at once the heavy night
Fell from my eyes and I could see,—
A drenched and dripping apple-tree,
A last long line of silver rain,
A sky grown clear and blue again.
And as I looked a quickening gust
Of wind blew up to me and thrust

Into my face a miracle
Of orchard-breath, and with the smell,—
I know not how such things can be!—
I breathed my soul back into me.
Ah! Up then from the ground sprang I
And hailed the earth with such a cry
As is not heard save from a man
Who has been dead, and lives again.
About the trees my arms I wound;
Like one gone mad I hugged the ground;
I raised my quivering arms on high;
I laughed and laughed into the sky,
Till at my throat a strangling sob
Caught fiercely, and a great heart-throb
Sent instant tears into my eyes;
O God, I cried, no dark disguise
Can e'er hereafter hide from me
Thy radiant identity!
Thou canst not move across the grass
But my quick eyes will see Thee pass,
Nor speak, however silently,
But my hushed voice will answer Thee.
I know the path that tells Thy way
Through the cool eve of every day;
God, I can push the grass apart
And lay my finger on Thy heart!

The world stands out on either side
No wider than the heart is wide;
Above the world is stretched the sky,—
No higher than the soul is high.
The heart can push the sea and land
Farther away on either hand;
The soul can split the sky in two,
And let the face of God shine through.
But East and West will pinch the heart
That can not keep them pushed apart;
And he whose soul is flat—the sky
Will cave in on him by and by.

Interim

The room is full of you!—As I came in
And closed the door behind me, all at once
A something in the air, intangible,
Yet stiff with meaning, struck my senses sick!—

Sharp, unfamiliar odors have destroyed
Each other room's dear personality.
The heavy scent of damp, funereal flowers,—
The very essence, hush-distilled, of Death—
Has strangled that habitual breath of home
Whose expiration leaves all houses dead;
And wheresoe'er I look is hideous change.
Save here. Here 'twas as if a weed-choked gate
Had opened at my touch, and I had stepped
Into some long-forgot, enchanted, strange,
Sweet garden of a thousand years ago
And suddenly thought, "I have been here before!"

You are not here. I know that you are gone,
And will not ever enter here again.
And yet it seems to me, if I should speak,
Your silent step must wake across the hall;
If I should turn my head, that your sweet eyes
Would kiss me from the door.—So short a time
To teach my life its transposition to
This difficult and unaccustomed key!—
The room is as you left it; your last touch—
A thoughtless pressure, knowing not itself
As saintly—hallows now each simple thing;
Hallows and glorifies, and glows between
The dust's grey fingers like a shielded light.

There is your book, just as you laid it down,
Face to the table,—I cannot believe
That you are gone!—Just then it seemed to me
You must be here. I almost laughed to think
How like reality the dream had been;
Yet knew before I laughed, and so was still.
That book, outspread, just as you laid it down!
Perhaps you thought, "I wonder what comes next,
And whether this or this will be the end";
So rose, and left it, thinking to return.

Perhaps that chair, when you arose and passed
Out of the room, rocked silently a while
Ere it again was still. When you were gone
Forever from the room, perhaps that chair,
Stirred by your movement, rocked a little while,
Silently, to and fro. . .

And here are the last words your fingers wrote,
Scrawled in broad characters across a page

In this brown book I gave you. Here your hand,
Guiding your rapid pen, moved up and down.
Here with a looping knot you crossed a "t",
And here another like it, just beyond
These two eccentric "e's". You were so small,
And wrote so brave a hand!
How strange it seems
That of all words these are the words you chose!
And yet a simple choice; you did not know
You would not write again. If you had known—
But then, it does not matter,—and indeed
If you had known there was so little time
You would have dropped your pen and come to me
And this page would be empty, and some phrase
Other than this would hold my wonder now.
Yet, since you could not know, and it befell
That these are the last words your fingers wrote,
There is a dignity some might not see
In this, "I picked the first sweet-pea to-day."
To-day! Was there an opening bud beside it
You left until to-morrow?—O my love,
The things that withered,—and you came not back!
That day you filled this circle of my arms
That now is empty. (O my empty life!)
That day—that day you picked the first sweet-pea,—
And brought it in to show me! I recall
With terrible distinctness how the smell
Of your cool gardens drifted in with you.
I know, you held it up for me to see
And flushed because I looked not at the flower,
But at your face; and when behind my look
You saw such unmistakable intent
You laughed and brushed your flower against my lips.
(You were the fairest thing God ever made,
I think.) And then your hands above my heart
Drew down its stem into a fastening,
And while your head was bent I kissed your hair.
I wonder if you knew. (Beloved hands!
Somehow I cannot seem to see them still.
Somehow I cannot seem to see the dust
In your bright hair.) What is the need of Heaven
When earth can be so sweet?—If only God
Had let us love,—and show the world the way!
Strange cancellings must ink th' eternal books
When love-crossed-out will bring the answer right!
That first sweet-pea! I wonder where it is.
It seems to me I laid it down somewhere,
And yet,—I am not sure. I am not sure,

Even, if it was white or pink; for then
'Twas much like any other flower to me,
Save that it was the first. I did not know,
Then, that it was the last. If I had known—
But then, it does not matter. Strange how few,
After all's said and done, the things that are
Of moment.
Few indeed! When I can make
Of ten small words a rope to hang the world!
"I had you and I have you now no more."
There, there it dangles,—where's the little truth
That can for long keep footing under that
When its slack syllables tighten to a thought?
Here, let me write it down! I wish to see
Just how a thing like that will look on paper!

"I had you and I have you now no more."

O little words, how can you run so straight
Across the page, beneath the weight you bear?
How can you fall apart, whom such a theme
Has bound together, and hereafter aid
In trivial expression, that have been
So hideously dignified?—Would God
That tearing you apart would tear the thread
I strung you on! Would God—O God, my mind
Stretches asunder on this merciless rack
Of imagery! O, let me sleep a while!
Would I could sleep, and wake to find me back
In that sweet summer afternoon with you.
Summer? 'Tis summer still by the calendar!
How easily could God, if He so willed,
Set back the world a little turn or two!
Correct its griefs, and bring its joys again!

We were so wholly one I had not thought
That we could die apart. I had not thought
That I could move,—and you be stiff and still!
That I could speak,—and you perforce be dumb!
I think our heart-strings were, like warp and woof
In some firm fabric, woven in and out;
Your golden filaments in fair design
Across my duller fibre. And to-day
The shining strip is rent; the exquisite
Fine pattern is destroyed; part of your heart
Aches in my breast; part of my heart lies chilled
In the damp earth with you. I have been torn
In two, and suffer for the rest of me.

What is my life to me? And what am I
To life,—a ship whose star has guttered out?
A Fear that in the deep night starts awake
Perpetually, to find its senses strained
Against the taut strings of the quivering air,
Awaiting the return of some dread chord?

Dark, Dark, is all I find for metaphor;
All else were contrast,—save that contrast's wall
Is down, and all opposed things flow together
Into a vast monotony, where night
And day, and frost and thaw, and death and life,
Are synonyms. What now—what now to me
Are all the jabbering birds and foolish flowers
That clutter up the world? You were my song!
Now, let discord scream! You were my flower!
Now let the world grow weeds! For I shall not
Plant things above your grave—(the common balm
Of the conventional woe for its own wound!)
Amid sensations rendered negative
By your elimination stands to-day,
Certain, unmixed, the element of grief;
I sorrow; and I shall not mock my truth
With travesties of suffering, nor seek
To effigy its incorporeal bulk
In little wry-faced images of woe.

I cannot call you back; and I desire
No utterance of my immaterial voice.
I cannot even turn my face this way
Or that, and say, "My face is turned to you";
I know not where you are, I do not know
If Heaven hold you or if earth transmute,
Body and soul, you into earth again;
But this I know:—not for one second's space
Shall I insult my sight with visionings
Such as the credulous crowd so eager-eyed
Beholds, self-conjured, in the empty air.
Let the world wail! Let drip its easy tears!
My sorrow shall be dumb!

—What do I say?
God! God!—God pity me! Am I gone mad
That I should spit upon a rosary?
Am I become so shrunken? Would to God
I too might feel that frenzied faith whose touch
Makes temporal the most enduring grief;
Though it must walk a while, as is its wont,

With wild lamenting! Would I too might weep
Where weeps the world and hangs its piteous wreaths
For its new dead! Not Truth, but Faith, it is
That keeps the world alive. If all at once
Faith were to slacken,—that unconscious faith
Which must, I know, yet be the corner-stone
Of all believing,—birds now flying fearless
Across would drop in terror to the earth;
Fishes would drown; and the all-governing reins
Would tangle in the frantic hands of God
And the worlds gallop headlong to destruction!

O God, I see it now, and my sick brain
Staggers and swoons! How often over me
Flashes this breathlessness of sudden sight
In which I see the universe unrolled
Before me like a scroll and read thereon
Chaos and Doom, where helpless planets whirl
Dizzily round and round and round and round,
Like tops across a table, gathering speed
With every spin, to waver on the edge
One instant—looking over—and the next
To shudder and lurch forward out of sight—

Ah, I am worn out—I am wearied out—
It is too much—I am but flesh and blood,
And I must sleep. Though you were dead again,
I am but flesh and blood and I must sleep.

The Suicide

"Curse thee, Life, I will live with thee no more!
Thou hast mocked me, starved me, beat my body sore!
And all for a pledge that was not pledged by me,
I have kissed thy crust and eaten sparingly
That I might eat again, and met thy sneers
With deprecations, and thy blows with tears,—
Aye, from thy glutted lash, glad, crawled away,
As if spent passion were a holiday!
And now I go. Nor threat, nor easy vow
Of tardy kindness can avail thee now
With me, whence fear and faith alike are flown;
Lonely I came, and I depart alone,
And know not where nor unto whom I go;
But that thou canst not follow me I know."

Thus I to Life, and ceased; but through my brain
My thought ran still, until I spake again:

"Ah, but I go not as I came,—no trace
Is mine to bear away of that old grace
I brought! I have been heated in thy fires,
Bent by thy hands, fashioned to thy desires,
Thy mark is on me! I am not the same
Nor ever more shall be, as when I came.
Ashes am I of all that once I seemed.
In me all's sunk that leapt, and all that dreamed
Is wakeful for alarm,—oh, shame to thee,
For the ill change that thou hast wrought in me,
Who laugh no more nor lift my throat to sing!
Ah, Life, I would have been a pleasant thing
To have about the house when I was grown
If thou hadst left my little joys alone!
I asked of thee no favor save this one:
That thou wouldst leave me playing in the sun!
And this thou didst deny, calling my name
Insistently, until I rose and came.
I saw the sun no more.—It were not well
So long on these unpleasant thoughts to dwell,
Need I arise to-morrow and renew
Again my hated tasks, but I am through
With all things save my thoughts and this one night,
So that in truth I seem already quite
Free and remote from thee,—I feel no haste
And no reluctance to depart; I taste
Merely, with thoughtful mien, an unknown draught,
That in a little while I shall have quaffed."

Thus I to Life, and ceased, and slightly smiled,
Looking at nothing; and my thin dreams filed
Before me one by one till once again
I set new words unto an old refrain:

"Treasures thou hast that never have been mine!
Warm lights in many a secret chamber shine
Of thy gaunt house, and gusts of song have blown
Like blossoms out to me that sat alone!
And I have waited well for thee to show
If any share were mine,—and now I go!
Nothing I leave, and if I naught attain
I shall but come into mine own again!"
Thus I to Life, and ceased, and spake no more,
But turning, straightway, sought a certain door
In the rear wall. Heavy it was, and low

And dark,—a way by which none e'er would go
That other exit had, and never knock
Was heard thereat,—bearing a curious lock
Some chance had shown me fashioned faultily,
Whereof Life held content the useless key,
And great coarse hinges, thick and rough with rust,
Whose sudden voice across a silence must,
I knew, be harsh and horrible to hear,—
A strange door, ugly like a dwarf.—So near
I came I felt upon my feet the chill
Of acid wind creeping across the sill.
So stood longtime, till over me at last
Came weariness, and all things other passed
To make it room; the still night drifted deep
Like snow about me, and I longed for sleep.

But, suddenly, marking the morning hour,
Bayed the deep-throated bell within the tower!
Startled, I raised my head,—and with a shout
Laid hold upon the latch,—and was without.

Ah, long-forgotten, well-remembered road,
Leading me back unto my old abode,
My father's house! There in the night I came,
And found them feasting, and all things the same
As they had been before. A splendour hung
Upon the walls, and such sweet songs were sung
As, echoing out of very long ago,
Had called me from the house of Life, I know.
So fair their raiment shone I looked in shame
On the unlovely garb in which I came;
Then straightway at my hesitancy mocked:
"It is my father's house!" I said and knocked;
And the door opened. To the shining crowd
Tattered and dark I entered, like a cloud,
Seeing no face but his; to him I crept,
And "Father!" I cried, and clasped his knees, and wept.
Ah, days of joy that followed! All alone
I wandered through the house. My own, my own,
My own to touch, my own to taste and smell,
All I had lacked so long and loved so well!
None shook me out of sleep, nor hushed my song,
Nor called me in from the sunlight all day long.

I know not when the wonder came to me
Of what my father's business might be,
And whither fared and on what errands bent
The tall and gracious messengers he sent.

Yet one day with no song from dawn till night
Wondering, I sat, and watched them out of sight.
And the next day I called; and on the third
Asked them if I might go,—but no one heard.
Then, sick with longing, I arose at last
And went unto my father,—in that vast
Chamber wherein he for so many years
Has sat, surrounded by his charts and spheres.
"Father," I said, "Father, I cannot play
The harp that thou didst give me, and all day
I sit in idleness, while to and fro
About me thy serene, grave servants go;
And I am weary of my lonely ease.
Better a perilous journey overseas
Away from thee, than this, the life I lead,
To sit all day in the sunshine like a weed
That grows to naught,—I love thee more than they
Who serve thee most; yet serve thee in no way.
Father, I beg of thee a little task
To dignify my days,—'tis all I ask
Forever, but forever, this denied,
I perish."
"Child," my father's voice replied,
"All things thy fancy hath desired of me
Thou hast received. I have prepared for thee
Within my house a spacious chamber, where
Are delicate things to handle and to wear,
And all these things are thine. Dost thou love song?
My minstrels shall attend thee all day long.
Or sigh for flowers? My fairest gardens stand
Open as fields to thee on every hand.
And all thy days this word shall hold the same:
No pleasure shalt thou lack that thou shalt name. .
But as for tasks—" he smiled, and shook his head;
"Thou hadst thy task, and laidst it by", he said.

God's World

O world, I cannot hold thee close enough!
Thy winds, thy wide grey skies!
Thy mists, that roll and rise!
Thy woods, this autumn day, that ache and sag
And all but cry with colour! That gaunt crag
To crush! To lift the lean of that black bluff!
World, World, I cannot get thee close enough!

Long have I known a glory in it all,
But never knew I this;
Here such a passion is
As stretcheth me apart,—Lord, I do fear
Thou'st made the world too beautiful this year;
My soul is all but out of me,—let fall
No burning leaf; prithee, let no bird call.

Afternoon on a Hill

I will be the gladdest thing
Under the sun!
I will touch a hundred flowers
And not pick one.

I will look at cliffs and clouds
With quiet eyes,
Watch the wind bow down the grass,
And the grass rise.

And when lights begin to show
Up from the town,
I will mark which must be mine,
And then start down!

Sorrow

Sorrow like a ceaseless rain
Beats upon my heart.
People twist and scream in pain,—
Dawn will find them still again;
This has neither wax nor wane,
Neither stop nor start.

People dress and go to town;
I sit in my chair.
All my thoughts are slow and brown:
Standing up or sitting down
Little matters, or what gown
Or what shoes I wear.

Tavern

I'll keep a little tavern
Below the high hill's crest,
Wherein all grey-eyed people
May set them down and rest.

There shall be plates a-plenty,
And mugs to melt the chill
Of all the grey-eyed people
Who happen up the hill.

There sound will sleep the traveller,
And dream his journey's end,
But I will rouse at midnight
The falling fire to tend.

Aye, 'tis a curious fancy—
But all the good I know
Was taught me out of two grey eyes
A long time ago.

Ashes of Life

Love has gone and left me and the days are all alike;
Eat I must, and sleep I will,—and would that night were here!
But ah!—to lie awake and hear the slow hours strike!
Would that it were day again!—with twilight near!

Love has gone and left me and I don't know what to do;
This or that or what you will is all the same to me;
But all the things that I begin I leave before I'm through,—
There's little use in anything as far as I can see.

Love has gone and left me,—and the neighbors knock and borrow,
And life goes on forever like the gnawing of a mouse,—
And to-morrow and to-morrow and to-morrow and to-morrow
There's this little street and this little house.

The Little Ghost

I knew her for a little ghost
That in my garden walked;
The wall is high—higher than most—

And the green gate was locked.

And yet I did not think of that
Till after she was gone—
I knew her by the broad white hat,
All ruffled, she had on.

By the dear ruffles round her feet,
By her small hands that hung
In their lace mitts, austere and sweet,
Her gown's white folds among.

I watched to see if she would stay,
What she would do—and oh!
She looked as if she liked the way
I let my garden grow!

She bent above my favourite mint
With conscious garden grace,
She smiled and smiled—there was no hint
Of sadness in her face.

She held her gown on either side
To let her slippers show,
And up the walk she went with pride,
The way great ladies go.

And where the wall is built in new
And is of ivy bare
She paused—then opened and passed through
A gate that once was there.

Kin to Sorrow

Am I kin to Sorrow,
That so oft
Falls the knocker of my door—
Neither loud nor soft,
But as long accustomed,
Under Sorrow's hand?
Marigolds around the step
And rosemary stand,
And then comes Sorrow—
And what does Sorrow care
For the rosemary
Or the marigolds there?

Am I kin to Sorrow?
Are we kin?
That so oft upon my door—
'Oh, come in'!

Three Songs of Shattering

I

The first rose on my rose-tree
Budded, bloomed, and shattered,
During sad days when to me
Nothing mattered.

Grief of grief has drained me clean;
Still it seems a pity
No one saw,—it must have been
Very pretty.

II

Let the little birds sing;
Let the little lambs play;
Spring is here; and so 'tis spring;—
But not in the old way!

I recall a place
Where a plum-tree grew;
There you lifted up your face,
And blossoms covered you.

If the little birds sing,
And the little lambs play,
Spring is here; and so 'tis spring—
But not in the old way!

III

All the dog-wood blossoms are underneath the tree!
Ere spring was going—ah, spring is gone!
And there comes no summer to the like of you and me,—
Blossom time is early, but no fruit sets on.

All the dog-wood blossoms are underneath the tree,

Browned at the edges, turned in a day;
And I would with all my heart they trimmed a mound for me,
And weeds were tall on all the paths that led that way!

The Shroud

Death, I say, my heart is bowed
Unto thine,—O mother!
This red gown will make a shroud
Good as any other!

(I, that would not wait to wear
My own bridal things,
In a dress dark as my hair
Made my answerings.

I, to-night, that till he came
Could not, could not wait,
In a gown as bright as flame
Held for them the gate.)

Death, I say, my heart is bowed
Unto thine,—O mother!
This red gown will make a shroud
Good as any other!

The Dream

Love, if I weep it will not matter,
And if you laugh I shall not care;
Foolish am I to think about it,
But it is good to feel you there.

Love, in my sleep I dreamed of waking,—
White and awful the moonlight reached
Over the floor, and somewhere, somewhere,
There was a shutter loose,—it screeched!

Swung in the wind,—and no wind blowing!—
I was afraid, and turned to you,
Put out my hand to you for comfort,—
And you were gone! Cold, cold as dew,

Under my hand the moonlight lay!

Love, if you laugh I shall not care,
But if I weep it will not matter,—
Ah, it is good to feel you there!

Indifference

I said,—for Love was laggard, O, Love was slow to come,—
"I'll hear his step and know his step when I am warm in bed;
But I'll never leave my pillow, though there be some
As would let him in—and take him in with tears!" I said.
I lay,—for Love was laggard, O, he came not until dawn,—
I lay and listened for his step and could not get to sleep;
And he found me at my window with my big cloak on,
All sorry with the tears some folks might weep!

Witch-Wife

She is neither pink nor pale,
And she never will be all mine;
She learned her hands in a fairy-tale,
And her mouth on a valentine.

She has more hair than she needs;
In the sun 'tis a woe to me!
And her voice is a string of colored beads,
Or steps leading into the sea.

She loves me all that she can,
And her ways to my ways resign;
But she was not made for any man,
And she never will be all mine.

Blight

Hard seeds of hate I planted
That should by now be grown,—
Rough stalks, and from thick stamens
A poisonous pollen blown,
And odors rank, unbreathable,
From dark corollas thrown!

At dawn from my damp garden

I shook the chilly dew;
The thin boughs locked behind me
That sprang to let me through;
The blossoms slept,—I sought a place
Where nothing lovely grew.

And there, when day was breaking,
I knelt and looked around:
The light was near, the silence
Was palpitant with sound;
I drew my hate from out my breast
And thrust it in the ground.

Oh, ye so fiercely tended,
Ye little seeds of hate!
I bent above your growing
Early and noon and late,
Yet are ye drooped and pitiful,—
I cannot rear ye straight!

The sun seeks out my garden,
No nook is left in shade,
No mist nor mold nor mildew
Endures on any blade,
Sweet rain slants under every bough:
Ye falter, and ye fade.

When the Year Grows Old

I cannot but remember
When the year grows old—
October—November—
How she disliked the cold!

She used to watch the swallows
Go down across the sky,
And turn from the window
With a little sharp sigh.

And often when the brown leaves
Were brittle on the ground,
And the wind in the chimney
Made a melancholy sound,

She had a look about her
That I wish I could forget—

The look of a scared thing
Sitting in a net!

Oh, beautiful at nightfall
The soft spitting snow!
And beautiful the bare boughs
Rubbing to and fro!

But the roaring of the fire,
And the warmth of fur,
And the boiling of the kettle
Were beautiful to her!

I cannot but remember
When the year grows old—
October—November—
How she disliked the cold!

Sonnets

I

Thou art not lovelier than lilacs,—no,
Nor honeysuckle; thou art not more fair
Than small white single poppies,—I can bear
Thy beauty; though I bend before thee, though
From left to right, not knowing where to go,
I turn my troubled eyes, nor here nor there
Find any refuge from thee, yet I swear
So has it been with mist,—with moonlight so.

Like him who day by day unto his draught
Of delicate poison adds him one drop more
Till he may drink unharmed the death of ten,
Even so, inured to beauty, who have quaffed
Each hour more deeply than the hour before,
I drink—and live—what has destroyed some men.

II

Time does not bring relief; you all have lied
Who told me time would ease me of my pain!
I miss him in the weeping of the rain;
I want him at the shrinking of the tide;
The old snows melt from every mountain-side,

And last year's leaves are smoke in every lane;
But last year's bitter loving must remain
Heaped on my heart, and my old thoughts abide!

There are a hundred places where I fear
To go,—so with his memory they brim!
And entering with relief some quiet place
Where never fell his foot or shone his face
I say, "There is no memory of him here!"
And so stand stricken, so remembering him!

III

Mindful of you the sodden earth in spring,
And all the flowers that in the springtime grow,
And dusty roads, and thistles, and the slow
Rising of the round moon, all throats that sing
The summer through, and each departing wing,
And all the nests that the bared branches show,
And all winds that in any weather blow,
And all the storms that the four seasons bring.

You go no more on your exultant feet
Up paths that only mist and morning knew,
Or watch the wind, or listen to the beat
Of a bird's wings too high in air to view,—
But you were something more than young and sweet
And fair,—and the long year remembers you.

IV

Not in this chamber only at my birth—
When the long hours of that mysterious night
Were over, and the morning was in sight—
I cried, but in strange places, steppe and firth
I have not seen, through alien grief and mirth;
And never shall one room contain me quite
Who in so many rooms first saw the light,
Child of all mothers, native of the earth.

So is no warmth for me at any fire
To-day, when the world's fire has burned so low;
I kneel, spending my breath in vain desire,
At that cold hearth which one time roared so strong,
And straighten back in weariness, and long
To gather up my little gods and go.

V

If I should learn, in some quite casual way,
That you were gone, not to return again—
Read from the back-page of a paper, say,
Held by a neighbor in a subway train,
How at the corner of this avenue
And such a street (so are the papers filled)
A hurrying man—who happened to be you—
At noon to-day had happened to be killed,
I should not cry aloud—I could not cry
Aloud, or wring my hands in such a place—
I should but watch the station lights rush by
With a more careful interest on my face,
Or raise my eyes and read with greater care
Where to store furs and how to treat the hair.

VI

Bluebeard

This door you might not open, and you did;
So enter now, and see for what slight thing
You are betrayed. . . . Here is no treasure hid,
No cauldron, no clear crystal mirroring
The sought-for truth, no heads of women slain
For greed like yours, no writhings of distress,
But only what you see. . . . Look yet again—
An empty room, cobwebbed and comfortless.
Yet this alone out of my life I kept
Unto myself, lest any know me quite;
And you did so profane me when you crept
Unto the threshold of this room to-night
That I must never more behold your face.
This now is yours. I seek another place.

Edna St Vincent Millay – A Short Biography

Edna St. Vincent Millay was born on 22nd February 1892 in Rockland, Maine, the eldest of three
daughters.

When she was 12, in 1904, her parents divorced. Although they had already been separated for some
years her mother, Cora, had found life raising three daughters with its domestic abuse and the

haphazard finances of a relationship with their father, Henry, too difficult. The four of them now moved from town to town, enduring various illnesses and living in poverty. Despite their circumstances their mother insisted on travelling with a trunk full of classic literature. Their one indulgence was to be able to read Shakespeare, Milton and other literary greats.

Edna did manage to keep up a remote relationship with her father thorough letters they sent each other for several years.

She loved the outdoors. One of her prime sources for poetic inspiration was Nature with its seasons of life and death, growth and decay. She would spend hours alone immersed in its company throughout her life.

After some time Cora and her daughters settled in a small house at the property of Cora's aunt in Camden, Maine. Finally with a semblance stability around her Edna began to write poetry. Her literary journey had begun.

All of the sisters were independently minded, speaking frankly and rubbing up against authority. Edna had decided she wished to be known as 'Vincent'. Her school principal in a display of petty authority called her by any other name that started with a 'V'.

Edna developed her literary talents at a furious rate. She began by being published in the Camden High School literary magazine, The Megunticook. At 14 she won the St. Nicholas Gold Badge for poetry, and by 15, she had published her poetry in the popular children's magazine St. Nicholas, the Camden Herald, and the high-profile anthology Current Literature.

In 1912, at the age of 20, she entered her poem 'Renascence' in The Lyric Year poetry contest. Despite being considered the best poem it was only given fourth place. The ensuing uproar brought Edna a lot of publicity. The winner, Orrick Johns, stated that 'Renascence' was the best poem, and that the 'award was as much an embarrassment to me as a triumph.' Another prize winner offered her his $250 prize money. In its aftermath the wealthy arts patron Caroline B. Dow heard Edna reciting her poetry and playing piano at the Whitehall Inn in Camden, Maine, and was so impressed that she offered to pay for her education at Vassar College.

By 1913, somewhat later than would be usual (she was 21) she entered Vassar College. She was not fully prepared for its strict regimen. The college expected its students to be refined and live according to their status as young women. Edna by now enjoyed the more liberal social aspects of life including drinking, smoking and flirting. She managed to combine both, continuing to write verse and also several plays.

She liberally engaged in relationships including several with women. She was keen to explore and experience more of life.

This experience included trenchant views on society and how it saw and valued women. During the years of the Great War Edna was an ardent pacifist, but her views on war would later change in a very dramatic fashion.

Edna graduated in 1917 and left for New York. Her life here was openly bisexual. Edna described her life as 'very, very poor and very, very merry.' This was evidently enhanced by her own natural beauty and frivolous nature, although these were only a mask to a more serious woman who was writing powerful poetry.

To provide income she worked with the Provincetown Players on Macdougal Street and the Theatre Guild.

Edna began to use her poetry, as she became more deeply engaged in feminist activism, to explore those themes. She soon had no hesitation in writing on subjects others found taboo.

She also had a remarkable way of gathering relationships and keeping her partners intensely loyal to her, even after, in the case of two suitors who happened to be literary critics, rejecting their marriage proposals.

Her ability to fall in and out of love together with the sometimes cold and raw New York environment seemed to move her poetry into shorter, pithier poems which were published in many magazines including Vanity Fair and the Forum

In 1919, she wrote the anti-war play 'Aria da Capo', which starred her sister Norma Millay and which played at the Provincetown Playhouse in New York City.

The following year, 1920, Edna published 'A Few Figs From Thistles'. Its subject matter of female sexuality and feminism was immediately criticized by many. But her reputation was only growing.

In January 1921 Europe beckoned and Edna went to Paris, where she met and befriended the sculptors Thelma Wood and Constantin Brancusi, the photographer Man Ray, and had various affairs. She also became pregnant. Although a marriage license was obtained Edna instead returned to New England where her mother helped induce an abortion with alkanet, as recommended in her old copy of 'Culpeper's Complete Herbal'.

Edna achieved significant fame when she won the Pulitzer Prize for Poetry in 1923 for 'The Ballad of the Harp-Weaver'. It was a magnificent triumph. She was also the third woman in six years to win this very prestigious award, following in the footsteps of Sara Teasdale (1918) and Margaret Widdemer (1919).

At a house party in Croton-on-Hudson, New York she met Eugen Jan Boissevain, a Dutch-born coffee importer. He was the widower of the labor lawyer and war correspondent Inez Milholland, a political icon Edna had met during her Vassar years.

On their wedding day a few months later, Edna fell ill with intestinal problems. Eugen drove her to Manhattan for emergency surgery. Edna, referring to her Pulitzer Prize, quipped, 'If I die now, at least I'll be immortal.' He nursed her back to health with remarkable devotion. He was a self-proclaimed feminist and encouraged her to write whilst he took care of everything else. Their marriage was open, and both took several lovers during its course.

In 1924 along with several others she helped to found the Cherry Lane Theater and its remit of staging experimental drama.

A further source of revenue was from short stories she wrote for the mass-market magazine Ainslee's. With these she stayed under the radar. To protect her poetic identity with its smaller and more serious audience, she used a pseudonym; Nancy Boyd. The publisher eventually offered to double her fees if he could use her real name. She refused.

In 1925, for $9000 they purchased 345 acres of farm and outbuildings called Steepletop near Austerlitz, New York, which had once been a blueberry farm, and then added another 300 acres. From a Sears Roebuck catalog kit they built a barn, and followed this with a writing cabin and a tennis court. Edna even found the time to grow her own vegetables.

Several years later they purchased Ragged Island in Casco Bay, Maine, as a summer retreat. Edna frequently had problems with the servants they employed and despite her liberal tendencies and social inclusiveness wrote 'The only people I really hate are servants. They are not really human beings at all.'

In the summer of 1936, Edna was riding in a station wagon when the door suddenly swung open. She was hurled into the pitch-darkness and rolled into a rock-strewn gully. She survived but with severely damaged nerves in her spine which required frequent surgeries and hospitalizations and at least daily doses of morphine. Edna was to live the rest of her life in pain.

By 1940 she was sufficiently alarmed by the rise of fascism to advocate for the U.S. to enter the war against the Axis powers. She later worked with the Writers' War Board and published a book of propaganda poems, 'Make Bright the Arrows: A 1940s Notebook', which managed to alienate even her most appreciative critics.

In 1942 in an article for The New York Times Magazine, Edna mourned the callous destruction of the Czechoslovak town of Lidice. Nazi forces had razed it to the ground, slaughtered its male inhabitants and scattered its surviving residents in retaliation for the assassination of Reinhard Heydrich. The article would serve as the basis of her 32-page poem, 'Murder of Lidice' in 1942.

In 1943, Edna was the sixth person and the second woman to be awarded the Frost Medal for her lifetime contribution to American poetry.

Despite the excellent sales of her books in the 1930s, her declining reputation, constant medical bills, and increasingly frequent demands from her mentally-ill sister Kathleen, meant that for most of her last years Edna was in debt to her publisher.

She did however quietly purchase a racing stable to indulge her passion for thoroughbred horse-racing. It would absorb much of her remaining income.

In 1949 after a twenty-six year marriage Boissevain died after a battle with lung cancer. Edna lived alone for the last year of her life. She drank heavily and lived almost as a recluse.

Edna St. Vincent Millay, after suffering a heart attack, fell down the stairs and died at her home on 19th October 1950. She was found approximately eight hours after her death. She was 58 years old.

She is buried alongside her husband at Steepletop, Austerlitz, New York.

Poems

Renascence & Other Poems (1917)
A Few Figs From Thistles: Poems & Four Sonnets (1920)
Second April (1921)
The Ballad of the Harp-Weaver (1922)
Poems (1923)
Distressing Dialogues, preface by Edna St. Vincent Millay (written as pseudonym Nancy Boyd) (1924)
The Buck in the Snow & Other Poems (1928)
Fatal Interview (Sonnets) (1931)
Wine from These Grapes (1934)
Conversation at Midnight (Narrative poem) (1937)
Huntsman, What Quarry? (1939)
There Are No Islands, Any More: Lines Written in Passion and in Deep Concern for England, France, and My Own Country (1940)
Make Bright the Arrows: 1940 Notebook (Poems) (1940)
The Murder of Lidice (Poem) (1942)
Second April and The Buck in the Snow, introduction by William Rose Benét (1950)
Mine the Harvest (Poems) (Edited by Norma Millay) (1954)

Translator

Flowers of Evil by Charles Baudelaire (with George Dillon) (1936)

Plays

Aria da capo (one-act play in verse; first produced in Greenwich Village, NY, December 5, 1919) (Also directed) (1921)
The Lamp and the Bell (Five-act play; first produced June 18, 1921)
Two Slatterns and a King: A Moral Interlude (1921)
Three Plays (Two Slatterns and a King, Aria da Capo, and The Lamp and the Bell) (1926)
The Princess Marries the Page (one-act play) (1932)

Opera

The King's Henchman (three-act play; New York, February 17, 1927) (Librettist)

Letters

Letters of Edna St. Vincent Millay (Edited by Allan Ross Macdougall) (1952)